We See Things Eye To Eye

Micah Moore

Presentation by *BookLeaf Publishing*

Web: www.bookleafpub.com

E-mail: info@bookleafpub.com

ISBN: 978-93-95890-80-9

First edition 2022

PREFACE

If any type of preface would suffice, there would be no point in the book. Let's dispense with the formalities and get into the meat of this book

A New Religion

Let's start a new religion;
Let's have a new beginning;
Let's make it our mission
To give it a good name.
Let's let others have their views;
Let's do this without the rules;
Let's see if the world gets used
To religion having a new taste.
If they can't, we won't make them;
True belief cannot be made in
A day. So if you want salvation,
I'd suggest taking the long way.

Bless The Flock

With idle incapacitation and hostility
Fueling my inspiration and possibility,
I explore the ins and outs
Of what I choose to be.
Crippling anticipation washes over me
And I become another sheep.
Let the reigns of indignation not fall upon me.
Let the rulers of the nation muzzle my ability
To waste the brain the good Lord gave me
On creativity.

I'm forced to worship moving pieces so fast I
Can't see. Was I prescribed the flies in my Eyes
from the powers that be?
Circling my head for so long, I begin to forget
What's right and what's wrong and I become
One of the flock.
I could be as white as snow, but you can only
See my flaws.
How did following the leader get us all so far
Away from where we are supposed to be?
I'd call for help, but all of us are lost

Brainstorm Breeze

You said I needed to relax,
So I was put under a rest
Hoping that a swift detachment
Would be enough to ease my stress.
I slept so long my brain went numb,
Now I'm as peaceful as a monk
But rest alone made senses dumb
And information piled like junk.
Nothing left to use my brain for,
Nothing more but rest and ease
And situations I had trained for
Blow away from brainstorm breeze

Control

What if I let one hand go
Limp in the sun releasing control?
Would it feel better than one
Straining to grasp at that same sun?
A planet in space revolves;
Another evolves and revolts. Substitute
Flesh for carbon, carbon for flesh: an
Organism living inside of a dish. Narratives
comfort, opinions vary but rarely; simply
The thought of purpose to our spinning
Gives hope. What desire is there to bear
The weight of that decision? Besides, the
Stars and galaxies aside, the universe is
Greek to me

Glass Jar

A gleam in my eye
May be a speck in yours.
Asleep in my mind,
Awakening at the source
Of my consciousness,
I'm careful to clear a way
As to not get lost in this
Long maze of entrails.
Scoop out my essence, and
Put it in a glass jar
On top of the fence that's
Surrounding the backyard
For the whole world to see;
I've got nothing to hide.
In a glass house, it's absurd
How one could choose to stay inside

Golden Rulebook

Can't you see my point of view
Just like you wanted others to
Do the same for you?
I guess the golden rule
Is meant to fetter you
Instead of better you.
I respect your perspective
But don't force direction
On the source of perception
Of those who walk the earth.
The silence they return is worth
More than you deserved

Harmony

Harmony, follow me
Until all you see is all of me.
Swallow me, hollow me;
Make me what I want to be.
Embarrassingly, barbarically,
Living through you vicariously.
Live no life, spend no time;
Seeing double, with half a mind to
Close the curtains to stop the hurting,
And keep my identity uncertain.
Leave again and I'll pretend
Like I know how to live again

Hope Is Not Knowing

Paint the letters on my eyes
So I can read them everyday
And see the world the way you want,
Though the world may want a different way.
Even if I'm well aware
That this worldview is false
I'd rather believe in something wrong
Than believe in nothing else at all.
If real belief is my obsession
And hope is truly the thing with feathers,
Then whether we all stay or go
Not knowing makes it all the better

I Wish I Could Trust My Gut

I wish I could trust my gut
As soon as I wake up
Because it always feels too good to be true;
Give 'er a few minutes and
She'll start eating away at me.
I wish I could trust my gut
As soon as I wake up
Because that guy is a different person;
His emotions, reactions, and frame of mind
Are something foreign to me.
How I wish I could trust my gut
As soon as I wake up,
But you can't trust a heavy sleeper

I'm Not A Statistic

I'm not a statistic, I am the equation;
I am a haven to the animalistic.
I'm not a trait, I am the instinct;
A life that is succinct in denying its fate.
I'm not ashamed, I am the shame;
I am the blame or at least to be blamed
For I am not lonely, I am alone.
As much of a home as home ever could be

Jim Crow

I shot Jim Crow
In the light of day:
Wings outline black,
Clouds outline gray.
Not much of a man,
No meat on his bones
With mouthful of daggers
And a gut filled with stone.
Fly if you want to,
But I know you can't.
Foundation is too soft,
No weight that can stand
Will be held in favor.
Shiny feathers, sleek
From blood with bullets in
His back and beak

Letters

Through ages of innovation
And millenia of civilization,
I still put pen to paper.
Ink bleeds through pages with a comforting
permanence.
Their words permeate matter, and time;
each carrying a moment into reality.
Within each pen stroke lies a fingerprint:
In each jot and tittle, an identity.
Why should we forsake such communication on
account of convenience?

Sent From iPhone

Mercurial Possession

Silver streams of mercury
Flow swiftly from my eyes
In an attempt to purge contempt
That's building up inside.
Selfish screams and bitter dreams
Can only help so much,
But the pain always remains;
I'm starting to lose touch
Of my humanity. How can it be
That hate has gotten the best of me?
I only dread that it will spread
To and through the rest of me.
Holding on to hate so long
Was the part where I went wrong;
What I needed was to relinquish
That anger that I've held so long

Mother Nature

There are buildings making clouds
Not a mile from my house;
Workers engage their precipitation.
They rely on machine's participation
To amplify Mother Nature's lamentations.
Nimble nimbus, float on by
Through miles of man-made morning sky.
Her groans grow louder, but nature's power
Cannot be paid by the hour

Pompeii

Show your love to the ash and dust
That is falling all around us.
How precipitous, Mount Vesuvius!
It's turned the sky into a rust.
It's turned my kind to piles of dust.
I've learned my eyes should never trust
For what floats like snowflakes burns with lust
To eat away at all of us

Quid Pro Quo

Give me a word
And I'll give you my ears.
Give me a sign
And I'll ask for direction.
Give me your worries
And I'll give you my fears.
Give me your hurt
And I'll offer protection.
Give me your tongue
And I'll put it in your cheek.
Give me a tool
And I'll put it to good use.
Give me your opinion
And I'll use it with what I think.
Give me your confusion
And I'll try not to get confused.
Give me your problems,
And I'll offer my help.
Give me a second,
And I'll give you all my time.
Give me a warning,
And I'll excuse myself.
Give me a look,
And I'll offer some hindsight.

Resurrection

I got out of bed today.
I suppose that's a step
In the right direction.
I spoke with a friend today.
There's a joy that comes with
A rekindled connection.
I'm out of my head today.
I could sure use a day
With no recollection.
I heard what you said to me
About breaking new ground
And feeling resurrection,
So I rose from the dead today

The Lord Is My Shepherd

The Lord is my shepherd;
I am no sheep.
Why should I keep
Myself from being better?
Would God not want more
From one in his image
Than bleating gibberish
Stuck among thorns?
The Lord is my teacher;
I'm a student, a pupil;
An eager observer who will
Follow the leader's
Actions. Did I get it
Twisted? Actions are louder
Than heaven is crowded.
Who could've missed this?

Three Little Pigs

Three little pigs,
"Sweet" little sausages;
Three bitter hostages
All cry for help.

One wolf for each,
Pigs go to market
Attempting to target
A price for each pelt.

None stayed home;
"This fur cannot suture,
It's off to the butcher
For this howling bunch".

Three little pigs,
Three little psychos
Stuffing their pie holes
With a perfect, pack lunch

The Powerful Irony

Please, tell me more
About what I should do;
You seem to know me
Even more so than you.
You spotted the speck
From your tower of ivory,
Yet it's you who can't see
The transparent irony.
How can you see
What I've already seen?
How can you be
What I've already been?
How can you judge
What you don't know yourself?
How are you spent
With what isn't your wealth?
Getting so bent
Out of shape isn't healthy.
This isn't your life,
But it may just as well be.

When Pigs Fly

As winged pigs
Step off of cliffs
To prove that swine can fly,
Can I have such faith
Like little babies
Dependent for their lives?
Can I be so bold
To test my soul
When I have the world to lose?
If pigs can fly,
Then why can't I?
We are but what we choose